Master Your Energy

Crystal Ermon

The Ermon Group

To my brother Timothy who stated
" We are only as great as the lowest amongst us"

And to the people who have helped me along the journey of spiritual awareness

A Spiritual Awakening ……………..…………..… 6

Meditation …………………………………….. 16

Your Perspective Creates Your Reality ………….. 19

Following Intuition & Finding Synchronicity ….. 23

Thought Journaling ………………………….… 29

Energy Is Real ……………………………….… 34

Tools: Amplify Your Energy ………………….… 39

Praise & Worship ……………………………... 43

Mastery ……………………………………….. 48

Preface

-Let me bring it back to my childhood for a second, just so you know where I'm coming from.

Growing up in Christianity my family religiously attended church every Wednesday and Sunday. As a child I was active in church activities I sang in the choir, praise danced, participated in church plays you name it, I was doing it. This was how my parents raised me and, for the most part, it had a positive impact on my upbringing. Fast forward, when I was 19 years old I had a realization after looking for a church to call my own. I was this devout Christian but I was broke. I was confused as to why I was so unlucky but followed every rule in the bible. I was kind to others, I prayed, I went to church I ministered to others. But somehow those mantras didn't help improve my lifestyle. There was still a missing ingredient and prayer and church weren't the end all be all to success. Finally, I had an epiphany I realized that If I wanted to experience some change in my life I would need to start with changing my beliefs. Even if that meant changing my belief in Jesus and God.

So, I decided to become an atheist, I played with the concept that maybe God didn't exist because he never answered my prayers and life kept getting worse. So I accepted the fact that if there isn't a God then I would take responsibility for creating the life that I wanted for myself. Now if you know Christianity (or any religion for that matter)to say God doesn't exist is pure blasphemy. Of course, my family flipped out and my mother and father spent countless conversations to bring me back to Christianity. They felt all their hard work raising me to be a Christian woman had gone down the drain. What I disliked about most Christians was that the church you attended was almost more important than your salvation. Everyone was constantly recruiting people to come to their church, and everyone believes that their church is "holier" than the next. I was disgusted with the church wars. It was clear to me that people completely forgot the true mission here on earth was to spread love.

My mind was set, I would find the truth on my own. I was going to take control of my life, I felt free and I began what I would call my spiritual journey. In life sometimes you have to remove yourself out of the equation just to solve the problem. So I started with a fresh slate, Godless, religion-less, and free on Sundays. I retracted from everything that was outside of myself to look inwards to find my spirit. With nothing but my intuition guiding me along the way. I went from being unaware of my power to mastering my energy to create my dream life.

This was the beginning of my spiritual journey. Most spiritual journeys come shortly after a spiritual awakening which is a life-changing experience for some people. First, you become more conscious of your place in the world and then you develop a new perspective on life. Things began to change within me and around me. The tricky part about it is once you awaken you can never go back asleep. Meaning you can't unlearn what you already know. That's what makes an awakening such a powerful experience. It is the knowledge a person gains from being aware of what life is all about. The veil is lifted and you can see that energy is real. It will cultivate change and spark inspiration to live a more authentic life. Now I understand why they say knowledge is power.

Over the time frame of 3 years, the mysteries of life became very clear to me. My whole life began to unfold in an auspicious way and at the time of this unfolding, it looked and felt like everything was crumbling around me. Over time I learned that in life everything may look as if it is falling apart but in all actuality, it is coming together, both processes require destruction. When I reflect on my life I can now see how my big picture was all coming together. I was 28 and living on the south side of Chicago and somehow I felt this inner urge to invoke change to do something new. I thought I could safely plan out the next stage in my life but the universe had something better in store. It was time to take a risk, some people would consider this to be crazy or irrational. I didn't do much planning I just got up and left Chicago. It was just me listening to my intuition and following God's voice while completely disregarding everyone around me. I was breaking free from the norm and moving to a new city in Atlanta Georgia.

During my first year in Atlanta, I would often journal my new understandings and experiences along my path. My Journal became a tool that helped me to make sense of the spiritual world & the magical things taking place in my life. I was growing and developing into the highest version of myself. I wanted to know who I was and I had dire need to discover my purpose in life. With no one to guide me, I relied heavily on my spiritual instincts to improve my life and it worked! It was during those journal sessions that the foundation for this book would be conceived.

ONE

A Spiritual Awakening

When the veil is lifted

Once you experience an awakening you become inspired to wake everyone else up! You feel compelled to tell everyone about this profound truth you now know. Well, unfortunately, you will find that others around you may not be ready to hear you out. In the beginning, people might look at you as if you're speaking another language. Don't let this bring you down just develop patience by respecting that we all have our separate journeys to walk. I decided to let my actions speak for me by switching up my lifestyle habits. A great philosopher, Epictetus stated,"Don't explain your philosophy. Embody it." The new me had to start evolving first. When the student is ready the teacher appears with this mantra you recognize when you are the teacher and when you are a student. So instead of waking up the friends and family that weren't ready for the knowledge I only gave it to the people who wanted to know. Don't cast your pearls before swine, means don't give knowledge and waste your words with people who don't value the message. I developed patience because I wasn't always aware, this was still all new to me so who am I to judge others who aren't ready. I was a meat-eater, a negative thinker, bug killer amongst many other things from my past. So don't be

too quick to judge others just because you have this new perspective on life.
I had to accept the isolation that came with my new mindset I didn't want to go through all of this magic alone and luckily I had my sister who was just as awakened. Having her along the journey helped me on the days when the world would make me feel like I was nuts!

I prayed to God to send me friends that were just like me that had experienced an awakening and he did. The cool thing about God was that he never left me he never let me fall and he always had my back. He knew that this journey was just going to strengthen my faith and prepare me for my life's purpose. Psalm 21-10 states "when my father and mother forsake me the Lord taketh me up". Don't be discouraged by the actions or comments from your family but find peace knowing that this is a part of your journey. Isolation is where growth happens. The struggle is where the character is built. Think of a seed, how it is buried in the ground where it is dark and all by itself. It is in this process of growth when it has broken above ground that it can feel the sunlight. All pain is temporary and when you emerge you will be a new version of yourself. The best version of yourself. The man/woman that you've always wanted to be.

The summer of 2016 is where it all started. I'm usually reserved when it comes to talking about this experience but it's the whole purpose of writing a book is to become an open book. So here goes nothing. This was the grand spiritual awakening as they call it. This was the first year I became conscious of energy, which was a term I was originally familiar with through science. I was prepared for this awakening from hanging around my "woke" friends that would drop knowledge to me from time to time. We all have those conscious friends that believe in all of those conspiracy theories lol. It was only a matter of time before the epiphany that would change my perception of the world forever. Throughout my life, my mind was always inquisitive putting clues together and wondering if life was really like The Truman Show movie, fake with everyone in it just playing a role. I would soon find out but let me break down how things happened in order...

It was lollapalooza week in Chicago and me and my siblings decided to turn up. Lollapalooza is one of the most lit weekends of the summer with over 20 artists and bands performing in Millennium Park. My sister and brother were having kickbacks at their crib so I decided to stay at their spot for the festivities. There were day parties and after-parties, the entire city was pretty much party central. My siblings and I all enjoyed having fun we were the life of the party.

There are many ways people experience an awakening; sometimes, it is forced through psychedelics, almost dying and seeing the light and through realization over a period of time. Your journey is yours to awaken to, and only you can experience it uniquely. Mine was a bit out of the box, I channeled a spirit, and luckily it was a nice loving one who empowered my friends and me. Everything was positive, and she showed us what negative energy was, and it was very cool, and we promised never to do psychedelics again. That's not what I'm here to promote, but I want to be honest with you all because I have integrity, and it won't allow me to leave that part out. Sorry, Ma!

Now, however, this understanding of your spirit self happens; you will learn that life is more than what meets the eye. You will understand that there are spirits all around us that we can't see. God made us this way in this dimension. He wanted us to learn to believe in what we couldn't see. Well, I cheated, and I ate the apple, so to say. I'm not proud of it, but somehow I feel that maybe I had to. Maybe God bent the rules when he sees how ratchet earth is becoming. Or perhaps I'm using that as an excuse to feel dignified. Either way, it happened, and I'm here to tell you about the life that unfolded for me in the years to follow. Here's to the spiritual awakening that changed my life. In a nutshell, here's what happened.

So I'm going to fast forward to the good part. One night my 2 siblings and our friend from New York and my brother's girlfriend were all home getting ready to go out. Our friend from New York suggested we do some sassafras before we head out. I was hella skeptical at first because I was usually the goody two shoes out of the crew but at the time I was going through a YOLO phases so I said lets try it. So he took out a Ziploc bag that had the powdery substance and he mixed it into a glass of water and we all drank it. They said it hits your system faster if you drink it. like 5 minutes later, boom! It hit us all we were all feeling it and immediately we all knew it was best to stay in and just vibe with the trip. We put some cool music on and just chilled. My vision started to allow me to see colors around everybody's body. I later found out that this color that surrounded us was called an Aura. In spiritualism, an aura is considered to be an energy field surrounding the body and is not visible to the naked eye. It was the coolest thing ever and then something out of this world happened.

We had channeled a spirit of some sort and she had an African or Caribbean accent. She was speaking to us and we all were silent and we all understood telepathically without saying a word. It was thee coolest thing ever. Omg. So much wisdom she was so positive and I learned so much from her in just that moment alone. I felt like it lasted for an hour or so. I learned that all names have meanings. She told one of our friends that my brother looked just like a Rafiki. And I was like how can someone "look like a Rafiki" it sounded like there was more to the phrase. The next day, after the drugs wore off, I went to look up Rafiki just to see if I was hallucinating or if our experience the prior night had substance. The name Rafiki to my surprise had a real meaning and it meant "friend". I really flipped out like wow this was not any regular high it was real. This also meant spirits were real. My whole world was different It could never be the same again and I didn't want it to be. I always knew there was something more to life, something big and some secret that everybody was kept blind to. After that night we all vowed to never take the drug sassafras again because it was very powerful and leaves you drained the next day. It was an experience we will never forget and changed our lives.

Summer 2016 resulted in new locations for us all. Everyone relocated and it's like we all had this urge to be in whatever city was calling us. My move was Atlanta, it reminded me of the mythical city that was called Atlantis, it was such a magical place. It is here that my spiritual growth occurred within a small network of people I would call my soul tribe. I considered it bootcamp, grounds for learning and growing and that was my permanent mood. It didn't take long before we were welcomed with a test of faith before landing a one-bedroom apartment in midtown. This complex was filled with some of the most interesting people. Our neighbors had the most unusual occupations a fire dancer, teacher, professional karaoke singer just to name a few of our new neighbors. I don't want to overwhelm you with the amount of sauce that the building had. But everyone was their own individual and being "weird" was cool, I knew these were the type of people I wanted to surround myself with. The first compliment I received at a neighbors kickback was " oh you have such beautiful aura, its pink! " those were the magic words that let me know the universe had a new type of crowd I would learn from. I was exactly where I needed to be my confirmation. An aura is a term used in spirituality to describe the human energy field which has a color emanation surrounding the body. Each color means something but we'll get into that a bit later.

The city of Atlanta was filled with high vibes because of all of the trees everywhere, land everywhere nature that surrounded us made it incomparable to the concrete jungle of Chicago. Peace was prevalent and you could hear yourself think if you come from a big city you know what I'm talking about. Little did I know this peaceful city was a great place that would improve my life forever.

I began my spiritual practices starting with meditation. Meditation is the practice of clearing thoughts and receiving clarity while focusing on your breathing cycles. After watching some youtube videos on how to meditate and what the benefits are. I attempted to give it a real try one afternoon. I started off with 10 min, then 20, then 45 min with meditation music at the last session. I felt so light and refreshed and I could find resolutions a lot quicker too. I was mad that I didn't know about this in the same way I learned about praying. I saw prayer as speaking to God while meditation was listening to him. Even the way we position our hands for prayer and meditation complement each other. In prayer, hands are together pointing upwards as if to send a message up to God while in meditation our hands or separate and open as if to receive a message. So it all made sense to me spiritually and logically.

Growing up I use to think negatively about meditation due to my parent's Christian teachings as a child. At first, I was skeptical but I had no problem researching the truth of the matter. Question everything and do your own research just to know for yourself. I had no friends to reference because they weren't into that stuff just yet. I found myself pioneering into a world I would have to learn on my own. I created my own study where I did a poll when I met successful people, I would ask them a personal question and see if they practiced meditation. To my surprise, many of them said yes. And every time I asked there was a look of surprise and intrigue on their faces. The gig was up! Finally, the secret was out! Think about all the celebrity interviews and how they frequently credit their success to everything but meditation. They credit it to hard work, never giving up, taking risks and God, But it was rare that I would hear any of the successful people talk about meditation. I began to think maybe this "secret" was more common than I thought,

Meditation soon became something I looked forward to every day. I had a lot of clearing to do and I enjoyed that clear understanding it gave me each time. At some point, you get over the awkward feeling of being in a quiet room by yourself with your eyes closed inhaling and exhaling. I had to get used to this quiet time but once I did it quickly became my favorite form of self-care. The clear thinking that came to me after each session is what kept me dedicated.

From listening to meditation music I learned that music carried vibrations and frequency that could be both positive or negative. These frequencies had either an effect on the subconscious mind. So listening to the positive frequency while meditating really lifted my mood, thoughts and made me feel happier. The healing frequency is said to be 432 hertz. I began to care about the frequency of music, my mental health, and my diet. I eventually made my way to being vegetarian as I learned more about spirituality. Eating high vibration foods put me in a better mood and I could think clearly. High vibration foods are foods that get their energy from the sun. Fruits and vegetables for the most part and lots of water. It was so hard to stick to this diet but I wanted to be a clear vessel for communication with God. It was honestly the best time of my life. Although some of my friends back home had a tough time accepting my new lifestyle, in Atlanta, it was completely the norm and there were tons of vegan shops all around me. Everyone there was "WOKE" so they embraced healthy eating. I read this book about shifting your paradigm and it gave me reasons to be vegetarian. Certain foods have spiritual health benefits and spiritual benefits. So I took the time to really learn the other purpose to be vegetarian outside of diet. I learned about the fluoride in our toothpaste and how it decalcifies your pineal gland. I learned how the Pineal gland was connected to the third eye which is called the all-knowing eye. I was becoming woke for real, for real.

My daily routine included waking up, sipping tea, meditating, writing in my journal, going outside for a jog and speaking positive affirmations every morning. I was disciplined in my journey and determined to improve my life. To achieve the level of spirituality meant for you it takes practice and dedication. Always being in the present moment in order to make the most of each day. The past is non-existent and the future is imagination the only reality that exists is in the now moment. Your power lies in the NOW and meditation is a catalyst for the present moment. They say when you are depressed it is because you are living in the past and when you anxious it is because you are living in the future but when you are at peace you are living in the present moment. New philosophies began to take president in my life and as long as it made sense logically and spiritually I listened to it. I had uncovered years and years of hidden knowledge and it was shifting my world. My thinking was changing, a new perspective on life was developing for me as my world began to shift in positive ways.

The spiritual journey is about unlearning the things you thought you knew. It's like a puzzle that you piece together day by day. So it takes a lot of patience you won't happen overnight for you. Trust the process and you will become more aware of the world around you. I learned that we are all one on this planet from the trees to the insect and animals. I felt connected in the circle of life. When before I felt superior as a human being I learned that every living creature co-exists on this planet together. I was a modern-day tree hugger. We all needed each other, the bees needed flowers and we needed honey. Become conscious of your role in the ecosystem so that you can serve humanity. I stopped littering and was just more loving to mother earth than I've ever been before. It was official I was a hippy who cared nothing more than to have harmony and peace on earth. When you feel this feeling you have opened your heart chakra, which allows you to have love energy for humankind, animals plants, and you feel deeply connected to them all. I knew this was real when I saw this willow tree get cut down and I couldn't help but feel compassion in my heart. For the first time ever in my life, I cried and felt really sad about that tree getting cut down. It was tragic to me and I vowed to do something about it.

Meditation was changing everything about me including my diet. I decided to become vegetarian and stopped drinking for a short period of time cleansing all impurities out of my system. My heart chakra was open and I felt love for animals, plant life and all people. As a pivotal point during the spiritual journey realizing that we are all one creates synergy in the world around you. for example, people get very frazzled when crossing paths with a bee especial when it gets very close to them, this is a common reaction out of the fear of being stung. After meditating I would see bees and not panic and simply move out of the way calmly and just like that it would leave me alone. I avoided the yelling and running and just understood that the bee is just flying living life and isn't intentionally trying to attack me. Little things like this open you up to harmony in the universe. I use to hate bugs and spiders but I soon understood the circle of life and I didn't want to kill any insects I would just simply place them outside. One time I saw a caterpillar crawling on my uncle's car window and I knew he was trying to make his way to the tree so I let him crawl on my hand and I placed him on a tree. Who was I becoming? Some modern-day humans who helped insects and saved trees and loved everyone unconditionally. This was the biggest turn around of my life and I embraced this new beginning.

Atlanta showed me the power of my thoughts and It took daily practice. I started at level 1 with nothing, zero, zilch. I gradually was on my way to manifesting everything I wanted and needed. This is how I learned the power that I possessed in the use of my thoughts and words. To improve your thinking you have to reprogram your mind and the way to do it is through reciting positive affirmations. Every morning I would listen to positive affirmation to get my day started. Here is a list of the affirmations I would repeat every day until it was embedded into my subconscious mind. You can find affirmations on Youtube or Google.

Today is a great day
Today is the best day of my life
Today I will notice only the good
My life is filled with an abundance of joy
Everything always works out for me
I follow the path of least resistance
I vibrate with the frequency of prosperity

and the list goes on.

I just summarized a year of experience in a couple of pages now for the remainder of this book I will break down other concepts and I'll revisit some of the things I mentioned. There is no rush to read this book. Take your time and just let it resonate with you. In no way am I promoting the use of psychedelics to achieve spiritual awakening. This just happened to be the path that was set for me. I want this book to be a way for you to experience your awakening in a way that is custom to your life path. In between chapters find time to practice some of the things I talk about so that the remaining chapters in this book will resonate with you.

TWO
Meditation

This is the most important part of mastering your energy. Meditation is the key to unlocking all sources of wisdom and clarity that stretch far beyond what humans can comprehend. With the understandings that are giving through deep inhaling and exhaling, we can achieve what they call bliss and it is that bliss that is open to consciousness and awareness of self and the outer self. Why meditate? Meditation allows you to perceive the world around you in a clear state. We can hear better, think more profoundly and be the best version of ourselves on a day to day basis. How long should I meditate? You should practice for at a minimum of 10 min daily or 30 min every few days if you choose to do so. The shorter the time frame the more days you should engage.

We live in a world that is constantly moving, constantly scrolling through social media, texting, constantly ready to prevent ourselves from experiencing boredom or stillness at all costs. What we fail to realize is that we a moving unconsciously in a drifting cycle that is leading us down a path of nothing but repeated cycles. When we take time to stop and be still we began to have a moment to reflect on our lives and what's happening in the life we live. Why is it so hard to sit in stillness? Why do we find it difficult to focus on nothing? These are the questions that will begin to bring you the answers you have been subconsciously running from. Our society aims to keep us so occupied with a bunch of nothing. Commercials cram your thoughts with ideas, fears, and temptations. Everywhere you go, your mind is being tugged at for attention all to keep you from living a life with purpose and intent. In a moving world, the code to unlock the matrix is in stillness and quietness.

The act of meditating as a practice of self-discipline and mindfulness has been around for centuries in the northern parts of the world and was later adopted by eastern civilization as a way to connect with higher frequencies. It is always about enlightening yourself so that you can become whole and achieve in life. Notice that I said achieve and left it open to specify exactly what it is you would desire to achieve. It is always about the viewpoint of the individual and it is a general understanding for all mindful people who decide to take up the path. It can be used to tap into other parts of the mind that otherwise wouldn't be used in our daily life. So it is a great tool to use when you are ready to be guided by the flow of nature and your mental state of being. Meditation can become addictive because it is such a peaceful feeling that is received afterward. It is recommended for both mental health and mental stability.

In our own lives, we can always find ways to take a moment of reflection to be in a mindful state. Meditation is just considering your mind and mental since these are parts of us that we so often neglect and leave on autopilot. We must take care of the mind because it is the engine that drives the brain and we all know how important the brain is to our bodily functions. How about we take our minds to a place of hope and into the gear of diving into a new perspective on life. Let us do it! Let us all make sure that our minds are just as kept up as our teeth and outer body which we care for on a daily. I don't think it will ever be acceptable to go not even a day without cleaning our teeth and because we use our mouths to talk so frequently. Almost just as frequently as we use our minds to think and daydream and get into our mode of focusing on a favorite TV show. Make your mind a priority like every other part of who you are. Let us sink into that self-care moment of truth.

Ok, this is how you meditate to achieve the best results. Throughout my studies, I've heard people come up with so many forms of meditation to get out of the stillness method. I have heard of shower meditation, meditation while exercising and many other forms that involve activity. We are hard-wired to move maybe because ADHD is a common disorder. Either way, I urge you to control your body and mind and not the other way around. Sitting with your legs crossed or in a comfortable position, eyes closed, inhaling through your nostrils and exhaling through your mouth (leave a small part between your lips).

Disclaimer: If you lay down on your back meditating you WILL fall asleep and it will become more of a nap than a meditation.

The meditative state is the sweet spot right in the middle of being awake and asleep and that's where you gain the conscious state of being.

There are some pretty phenomenal things you experience the more you meditate and the longer you sit in stillness. Be sure to find a space that is dim with a small amount of light, preferably no light. When your eyes are closed and you have been meditating for about a week or so reaching up to 30 minutes in a meditation session you will begin to see purple swirls. They take the shape of a spiraling effect. Once you have passed through this part of meditation your vision will then fade into a space of darkness with stars and it will look as if you are floating through the galaxy. It coins at the phrase the Youniverse is within us. And if you look at the brain's nervous system it is identical to the stars in the galaxy. Mac Miller did a great depiction of this in his music video " Fight the feeling" where he shows inside the mind in a meditative state and It was complete darkness and one by one little dots of light pop up and eventually stars fill up the dark space. It is the most amazing experience. This is what the journey inwards looks like.

So if you want to be able to understand the following chapters to some extent it will require you to meditate. I strongly suggest it so that it will be like a guide throughout your journey. Experience is the only teacher when it comes to spiritual growth. There are no short-cuts on this side of the fence.

THREE
Your Perspective Creates Your Reality

Mastery is involved when it comes to perception. Only you see the world the way you do, others see it differently. Only you can envision the past and future events, others cannot. Our past shapes our future and our present creates it. Right, this moment you are creating the next 30 minutes with the power of your intent. You are also creating for the future by choosing to be perceived in a way by others. If you wish to receive a check then act like you did and plan like you did and in this time frame a check will appear. And people will use their belief in you to believe more. You altar your future when you perceive your situation as a method to gain money and a powerful manifestation of having what you wish. This is how it works, You are loveable and if you feel love then love will find you. You are wise if you teach then wisdom will flow. You are protected if you feel safe life will shield you, so perception is greatly influenced by emotions. Also altered by emotions and the way we interpret them.

Perspective is what changes the way you see the world, and it affects your demeanor. Once your demeanor changes you will change the circumstances of your reality. It's that simple. Life has always been about how you see the world, how you see yourself, and the world responds to this.

Reality is only an illusion because we assume it is based on facts when it is based on us! We are the ones who determine what gives life meaning we create the definition. But only a healthy mindset. Please be sure to have a healthy mind that is not mentally ill so your perception can be clear and true to you. Once you are operating from a healthy mental state you are more than equipped to engage in the mind-controlling of what life can offer you. We all must take out time to facilitate mental health check-ups so that we know our world is being perceived correctly. This is what matters most in this step. Once we have a clear healthy mind we can operate in our world in a way that will benefit us holistically and generate the mechanisms it takes to change the reality we live in.

From Lack to Abundance

Perspective hack #1. Thinking of all of the things you can't do or don't have can leave you feeling discouraged or down and out. The cure for shifting your perspective from lack to abundance is gratitude. Show the universe you are grateful and you will be given more to be grateful for. So look around your living space and began to take inventory of how much you do have and count the simplest of things. For women bobby pins and rubber bands can have a girl feeling bountiful. I'm sure you've got a ton of something in your house. Do the same with your finances instead of focusing on what you can't buy think of all the things you can buy with the funds you have. What can you buy? We can begin to appreciate how much we do have when we choose to count our blessings. Here's a great exercise to increase your abundance flow.

Gratitude List:

I am thankful for being alive
I am thankful for a healthy body
I am thankful for nice clothes
I appreciate my loving family
I am grateful for my job
I am grateful for money in my account
I am thankful for delicious food to eat
I am grateful for legs to walk
I am thankful for eyes to see clearly
I appreciate my loving relationship

A gratitude list will put everything in focus for you changing the way you see your world. Giving you a true sense of all that you have to be grateful for. We do so many things automatically we forget that to walk or to breathe or to type are blessings that we sometimes take for granted.

Act As If

Perspective hack #2. The next uber or lyft you take choose to see yourself as a successful (insert dream job) with a personal chauffeur. As you align with this perspective watch how your posture improves and your emotions change. This is you aligning with the higher version of yourself. One time I was out with my two of my male friends and I played with the perception that I had two bodyguards. Now, of course, don't make a public announcement about what you perceive because this is all about your mind, you only need to think about it. Your mind will react to these thoughts and it will alter your mannerisms, voice tones, and posture. Utilize this to build your confidence and practice creating your reality, not for self-delusion but self-awareness.

Positive Possibility

Perspective hack #3. A weekly routine of mine is to create a list of positive possibilities. This is great to apply to an important day coming up, challenging situations, crises, trips, etc. The purpose of this exercise is to create a positive outcome. I usually list 10-20 possible scenarios that are all positive. You can make your list as long as you want. Below you can see the example given to help you construct your list.

Scenario: "I want to go to Paris fashion week, but I don't have the funds"

Positive Possibilities (literally write this as the header, let it be known in the universe your intentions)

I win an all-expense-paid trip to Paris
I gain new clients this week and make more than the money I need for my trip
My friend who owns a private jet gives me a super discounted flight rate
I run into a designer who wants to book me in a runway show
I have an amazing time in Paris
My radio friend shows me all the cool hip places in Paris

My french speech drastically improves
I have the cutest outfits from my trip
I get signed to a modeling agency in Paris
Everything works out better than expected

Notice the perspective each positive possibility gave me. Possibility number one is from the perspective of starting with no money and just lucked up on a free trip. While possibility number two is from the perspective that I get new clients to make the money needed. Each possibility listed is assuming that there is progress being made towards the trip. From making money to using it for discounted flights, to having an amazing time in Paris. This is a positive possibility that assumes that my trip comes to fruition. Cover all the basics of your situation and think of it from the beginning to the end.

Use this exercise anytime you wish to change your perspective from negative to positive. After you have completed your list go back and read it (quietly or out loud) once or twice a day. If you find yourself slipping into a state of doubt and worry encourage yourself by reading over the list. This is a way to keep your thoughts on track with the outcomes you prefer to experience. I should warn you not to be obsessive reading every hour but to feel relaxed and confident in knowing that good things are coming your way. Feel emotions of excitement and gratitude for things working out better than expected.

You might find yourself feeling inspired to take action in the direction of the statements made on your list. Look at how the first possibility states that I could win a trip. The inspired action from that would be signing up for promotions that advertise free trips to Paris. This can happen in one or two ways. You can search for a trip give always or you could just let them come to you in the form of an ad randomly popping up on social media or in your email. Magical little things like this can and will happen.

FOUR
Following Intuition and Finding Synchronicity

It is in the form of intuition that God gives us knowledge, understanding, and forward-thinking, you can predict what is to come if you tap into your emotions. It isn't about being a know it all but knowing from a sense of self-awareness. Your body's energy field is advanced and can sense when good energy and bad energy is on its way to you or in your presence. Babies have no control over their energy field or emotions. That is why they are excellent detectors of or sensing danger nearby.

Use intuition to guide you and to know what to do. It's ok to be confident in knowing before actualizing the event. We don't always need to witness the things we sense are coming if it is not for our highest good. Life is here to teach us about who we are. How are you moving through this world, what is guiding you? Is it your ego? Is it the suggestions of others? Or can you find the internal navigation that is inside of yourself and let that be your compass. With the combination of meditation, you can hear the intuitive nudges you receive clearly. Peeling back layers of misguided thought patterns meditation will bring you to the core of who you are.

The way to open up to receive more miracles is by following your intuition and going with its flow. I know this can sound odd because we are so accustomed to schedules, planning, and commitments. Trust in a higher power that knows where you are in correlation to everything you want to achieve. God has a bird's eye view of our life, and unfortunately, we can only see what is in front of us. You'll discover that sometimes what you planned for the day will not be the thing that leads you to your pot of goals. Your pot of goal is whatever you want in your life, whether its happiness, love, increased finances the list goes on. This is how it works, you have to believe that miracles are real, be guided by your intuition, and then you have to trust life. This can be easy if you practice it daily. I spent a day to give this theory a try. I had a feeling about what I wanted to do and went the flow. It can be something as simple as going to Starbucks to get a coffee. The Universe would then have me run into someone on the way there, and maybe our conversation would be an answer to a question I had earlier. Or I would go to Starbucks and then see a shop or a park and get the impulse to go there instead. It's all about flow and always being open to your destination changing, the Universe just wants to get you up and out of the house and headed in the right direction. So follow each impulse like a crumb trail until it leads you to a final destination. You will know when you have arrived, there will be confirmation. You might meet someone relevant to what you are working on, or you might end up signing up for something that you've been meaning to do. Whatever the case is, you will find it, and it will find you. This is the easiest way to witness the magic that exists in the world.

How much time in your day do you have to wonder and explore? Feel free to use an affirmation for your day " Today will turn out better than expected." Allow yourself to naturally be drawn to the people and places that are meant for you. You don't know who or what they are, but somehow the Universe does, so just go with it. Go with whatever you feel you should do, even if that includes canceling on friends. If your vibe tells you to cancel on Brittany, then cancel on her and go and hang with who you have a vibe to. Follow your instincts. Don't be afraid to do what you feel is best for you. To really walk the spiritual path, you must be willing to leave people behind. Your loyalty is not to anyone but yourself and God; he knows the way. Trust him and trust yourself.

It is our human nature to want to control by planning every single event down to the minute. There is something about plans and schedules that brings us great comfort. Did you know you can create your days without set plans? We can sometimes feel lost with nothing to do, most people won't leave home unless they have a reason to. Find time to have days that are not planned and let your day create itself along the way. When you journey into the unknown, you'll always be in the right place at the right time. Nothing will be set in stone because you're open to the flow of the Universe, allowing the most unexpected things to happen for you. Make it fun, and see it as adventuring into the world, see the world as an experience by looking at something with childlike eyes! Be excited and keen to where your instincts nudge you to be. Even if it seems silly to go to a particular store or wherever you lead to. Go and know that there's got to be a piece of the puzzle waiting for you. It's about finding the articles to your puzzle and finding the crumb trail that will lead to your goals. Get out of your comfort zone and go for it. Each of us has our own path to be brave and walk. Often times, you will walk on your path alone. Don't fear this embrace it as apart of growth.

Intuition is having the time of day to explore what your inner self wants to do. When you do it, it will sync you with experiences that are all close in proximity or similar to your thoughts. So it is the universal way of connecting dots. Listen to your heart, and it will guide you to synchronicity close by. What makes this magical fact that no matter where you are in life, there is always a dot waiting to connect you to the next step on your path. Synchronicity is the exact opposite of coincidence, and those are just things that make no sense together. It almost like saying the Universe didn't know that you were matching up with your desires like oops! Didn't see that coming must be a coincidence, our bad. Yea, so that doesn't exist on the spiritual side of the world. Change your vocabulary and give yourself credit that you are following your path, and things are looking up for you. This isn't chance happening; this is destiny.

Magic is precedent when we show ourselves receptive to the energies in the world. Once you have succeeded in listening and following and acknowledging, you will then receive a signaling message called angel numbers. These are numbers dating back to the beginning of time syncing present experiences with future experiences, and together they create messages from angels. If you believe in angels, this is going to be an easy concept to receive. If you don't know then I won't make you a believer, you will have to experience the hand of God and his angels' presence in your own journey and only then will you know and believe. But in the meantime, here's what angel numbers mean to us and our lives.

When walking into a store, for no apparent reason, you will find yourself looking in a direction. Very noticeably, you will see a number that, for some reason, stands out to you. This is a message for you to find the meaning of it. A universal communication code, yes, I know sounds like a movie scene, but it is real, our world has always had more to it than what meets the eye. You are now being guided in every form that guidance can come. You are following your intuition, listening to yourself and knowing that you are in the right place thanks to synchronicity. And the angel numbers are giving you directions to follow. The message will resonate with you, and that is the proof in the pudding. Each word that you receive is always going to be of relevance to your life, and you will laugh because it will be so on point. There is no denying that God is real. He is not a fairytale myth or magician. He is a practical guide and is showing you the hand he has in your life.

You might look at the time during this book and catch repeated numbers like 1:11, 2:22, 4:44, and so on. These numbers are not only clear indicators of the magic occurring in your life, but these numbers are considered to be angel numbers, and this how they communicate with us. These are the signs of ultimate synchronicity, and it will always be at the most auspicious times that you catch them. You might find these repeated numbers during a meaningful conversation, or maybe during your travel somewhere, you'll look up, and they will be there. You'll go to the grocery store, and your total will be $7.77 or another triple number. These are just some of the common ways you catch specific numbers. There is something that makes you look at the clock at a particular time, it is instinctual. In Numerology, the divine science of numbers, it is understood that each name carries a specific vibrational meaning.

When I first learned about Numerology, it was during a supernatural experience. At the same time, I was sleeping, I felt myself pulling out of my body, not sure if I was going to astral project or not but I was so scared that I woke up and the first thing I saw was the time on my phone, 4:20 am. I quickly went to google and searched 420 angel numbers and read the meaning. Angel number 420 meant that the angels were trying to communicate with me. I thought this was so crazy, but after the experience in my sleep, I could only assume it had some truth to it. So I texted my brother the only other spiritual person I could tell at the time, and he broke down to me what I experienced. I thought I wanted to astral project, but I was too afraid, which was an indicator I needed to clear myself of fear altogether. Overall this was my first encounter with angel numbers, and I'll never forget it. Here are more numbers and their meanings. All angel numbers can be researched, and they all have a purpose for your situation. Find time to research this subject independently. More information is available on youtube, google, and Instagram. It also has lots of spiritual pages you can follow that will teach you more about the subject of angel numbers.

111 your intentions are manifesting quickly ! make sure you're focusing on what you actually want, not what you don't want.
222 Stop worrying everything is working out just as it's supposed to. Trust that you are on the right path.
333 The ascended masters are right by you, assisting you with whatever it is that you're currently working on. You're in great hands.
444 You are entirely surrounded by angels. You are being guided through whatever you are focusing on.
555 HUGE changes are up ahead. Trust that this transition for your highest good. Prepare for massive shifts! Things are getting exciting.
666 Your thoughts need some refocusing. This is a reminder that you are a spiritual being having a human experience. Reconnect with your spirituality.
777 Luck is on your side. You are on the ultimate spiritual path. Keep doing what you're doing.
888 Lots of money. Financial abundance is on its way to you right now. You are aligned with the money you desire
999 You are being nudged to finish something because that completion will unlock the next step for you.
1111 You are on the right path. You're a master manifestor and know precisely where you're going. Alignment at it's finest.
000 New beginnings. A fresh start. Being one with the Universe. A reminder that you are the creator of your own destiny.

There will be other number sequences that catch your eye, and when they do come to your attention, just look up what they mean. Pay attention to the thoughts you have when you see them because the message you receive will relate to that.

As you read the knowledge provided to you in this book, it will soon resonate with every part of who you are and slowly layer by layer. You will be receptive to the magic surrounding you. There is no need to rush through this book give the universe time to show and tell you its truths. Right place, the right time will be a new mantra for you. This book isn't about finishing it but more so about growing spiritually, and that takes time. As an entrepreneur, I had dreams and goals that I wanted to happen quickly. But what I learned is that my personal and spiritual journey was tied into the growth of my business. I tried to reach those levels of understanding enlightenment so severely. Still, the time had to take its course and teach me through experiences. Life experiences can't be rushed patiently wait for situations to arise so that you can learn from them. I use to despise the saying that patience is a virtue, and it is because growth is gradual; it doesn't happen overnight, or it would be creepy lol. It's just like a baby who is currently eating mushy baby food. However, they might want to eat all the delicious food adults eat, their bodies aren't equipped to digest it. Over time the baby develops teeth, and it becomes more provided to bite into more solid foods. So just like the baby, we must develop patience so that we can grow and be prepared for the next stage in our lives.

FIVE
Thought Journaling

"I don't know what I think until I write it down" - Joan Didion (author and American essayist)

Here's for a self-check-in! Have you ever conducted a self-evaluation to see what's going on with you? I'm referring to internally, externally, mentally, emotionally, etc. If this seems complicated to pinpoint, you might want to consider adding journaling as a new habit. The power of writing is excellent for your mental health. It's like a brain dump where you can unload all of the thoughts going on in your head in a safe and controlled environment. It's better than word vomit when you vent your frustration onto your friends or coworkers. By doing this, you might subject yourself to unwanted feedback or judgment. Mainly because the people you choose to vent to may not have the mental capacity to take in your issues.

Journaling is the single most thought-provoking tool that helps you monitor your energy. If there is a time when you want to harness your personal power through thought, writing things out will give you the freedom to challenge yourself creatively. What are you thinking? If you understand that your thoughts are powerful enough to create energy, then you would be mindful and create more intentionally. It is easy to think and even more comfortable to think the wrong thoughts. Master your thoughts by monitoring who you are being perceived as by yourself. You are also a perceiver, you hear the thoughts you think. So don't let them auto-generate. Make it a habit to consciously review what is going on up there in your head. Journaling isn't about missing people and writing about how much you miss them, it is about observing why you miss them. Can you see the difference in the approach? Be the observer ask yourself why, how, and what, and there will be more clarity to gain.

The tools needed for journaling are relatively inexpensive. It would help if you had paper, a pen, and a quiet space to write uninterrupted. Be present and think for yourself. When writing the date, the page and you can add the time and also title the subject your writing about so that when you revisit the topic, you can see how you've grown.

Throughout childhood, you might have remembered having a diary where you wrote about things that happened at school or at camp. I often used it to write about my crushes (laughable) when I think back on it. A journal's purpose is very different from a diary. It isn't about writing for each day. Journals are about the big picture, themes that are playing out in your life, and something to reflect upon. Organize and title each journal giving it a topic that is relevant in your life to show a completed chapter in your life. I include the year on the front of the notebook; this helps keep a record of an epiphany or solutions that arise.

Having this clarity helps us move forward to the next phase of our life with time we can process it gradually. There is no need to rush to the answer journaling allows information to unfold at a pace specific to your personal development.

Journal to manifest the life you want, you know what they say, when you write it down, it becomes real, and this is true. So use this journal as more than just a thought book but put the thoughts you enjoy dreaming about, watch how you fine-tune the things you "think" you want in your life. There is something about seeing your dreams written out that allows you to revise it in a way that appeals to your honest intentions. It's like when we make rude jokes, it can be funny, but it looks horrible if you write it out. So use this practice to decide what you really want for your life and allow time to let the dreams manifest.

Don't worry if you aren't the most excellent writer. This isn't about writing for a grade; no one is checking this journal but you. It is private and should only be read by you. Also, be fair and write only when you are inspired to do so. If you find that you are lazy, then force yourself the first couple of journal entries. Give it a shot to be fair to your person.

Remember, this is all about energy, the power of writing is amplified based on your ink color. We write daily with black, blue, and seldom red ink, we should adhere to the importance that ink color has on writing. Black ink has very dominant but neutral energy, which is why it is more commonly used. Blue ink has high strength, so it should be used when writing goals, and when we are creating a list of desires we wish to fulfill. Use blue in with positive intentions. Don't write about the horrible day at work only to amplify that energy. Not a good idea. Use red to write about subjects of great importance and seriousness. Use red sparingly; it is genuinely unnecessary unless you are writing a deadline date.

Here is an example of a journal entry format. This is also what I personally use as well as many others, I find it to be the most effective journal style.

November 17, 2019

Gratitude
I'm thankful for the clarity I have been receiving. I'm grateful for the confidence to speak my truth. I'm thankful for the new business opportunities. I'm thankful that both of my parents are still living. I'm grateful for the clarity that I have on how to move forward. I'm grateful for my new workout routine.

Affirmation
Today is the best day of my life! Today I will complete everything on my to-do list. Today I will try something new. Today I will commit myself to be more loving and kind to others. Today I will open a private bank account. Today I will finish my presentation. Today I will excel at all that I do. Today I will call Adam and go over the new marketing plan.

New ideas:
To write a book that is clear, concise, and to the point. To reach out to book clubs in the surrounding areas and connect.

Daily Reflection: 7:30 pm

Today was really chill, and I got a lot done. I went to the bank and learned that I only need $250,000 to open a private bank account. I'm glad I'm finally planning things out in advance. It gives me so much space to adjust, and I'm not rushing things like I used to. I'm learning to let go of the addiction to last-minute adrenaline. I want to have a chill pace to life. Planning is apart of maturing, and that is apart of my growth. I got out of the house for a little bit and did something I haven't done in years, I went to the library and checked out some books. They had some flyers for free meals on Thanksgiving, I took a stack and decided to pass them out to homeless people in the area. Giving isn't always about what I have. I'm learning it's about thinking of others. I'm glad I have Adam in my corner. He always comes through in the clutch. I'm so ready to roll out this new marketing plan, but it's def looking like a headache. I wonder how it's all going to pan out. Hopefully, a miracle happens just when I need it. Ah, today was smooth.

That is the format I use for my daily journaling. Here is the format for thought journaling.

November 17, 2019

Writing for clarity
It is clear to me that I will be buying my first home, and when I think about it, I wrote about buying home last year in my 2020 goals. So it makes sense that the future is now the present moment. For the longest, I had this warped idea that to have a house without a husband was backward. Maybe those are just ideas that I learned from my Dad. He once told me that a woman living in a house by herself will attract thieves and danger lol. I was thinking today, hey, that's not right, a house is really a great way to make money. Here in Hollywood, there are tons of opportunities for renting your property out for movies, air bnb , tenants, peerspace, and more. I guess I just had to lose the fear and gain a new perspective before I could see that this is it, my time is now. Everything is falling in place if I think about it. I learned that I could use my private bank account to leverage my home loan. Then I started to see it as an investment instead of an expense. I'm so ready. I see the big picture, finally.

So writing would allow the answers to unravel and come to realizations. Writing for clarity puts the doubts on paper and all of the confidence on paper and chooses what's right to you. It also marks life events that are taking place and helps you to move past them. You will notice if you are writing about the same subject multiple times. It will help you to push past events so that you can make forward progress. Anything from emotional themes of love and relationships, business and career, and personality improvements. You will make an effort to evolve if for nothing else but to write about a new subject in your life.

SIX
Energy Is Real

Energy is real because if you are near enough static, you will get shocked, right? It's about you and your "vibes." so if this is real, then why can't we see it? And if it's real, then how can we tell the difference between good or bad energy? Well, here goes the grand slam! Boom! Power is the most practical thing on this planet. There are different types of negative energy and stagnant energy, kinetic energy. In this chapter, you will discover the power you have and the energy of those who occupy space in your life. In the beginning, God created the heavens and the earth, and he spoke the word of energy, and things were.

Life is all about maneuvering through the pattern of waves that energy creates. Let us say, for instance. You are walking in a park, and along comes this fox dressed in sheep's clothing pretending or appearing to an innocent but there is a vicious vibe that comes over you like a wave, and you see the sheep with your eyes, but the energy is telling you it's a fox in sheep's clothing. That's what energy does. It tells the truth. Unwavered by the fox's desire to cover up with fakeness. It will yell at you and say," Hello! Here I am the energy of negativity. " Hello, here I am, the energy of positivity." You just have to be aware enough to listen to your intuition.

You might brush it off and say your just tripping or being judgmental. But there is a difference between being a judgemental person and making a judgment call. We are living in times were we crucify the people who are "judgmental" because no one wants to be that. These two words are often confused, but here's the breakdown. The term Judgemental means to display an excessively critical point of view. To make a judgment is the ability to make considered decisions or come to sensible conclusions. You are entitled to make judgment calls in regards to your life. It is healthy for your well being and is needed when meeting new people, going new places, doing a business deal, etc. We are all constantly making judgment calls throughout our lives, not because we were judgmental, but because of it necessary for survival.

Being aware of energy will not only keep you from harm's way but allow you to see persons' true colors and detecting whether someone's energy is dark or light can save your life. Some people possess dark power and mask it with good looks, charm, positive words, and acts of kindness. Generally, we tend to look at things on a surface level while dismissing the vibes we feel around a person or place. It is not always easy to pinpoint these things because it will appear to be a small character flaw. And when we don't trust ourselves enough to identify those flaws, we are subconsciously choosing to be deceived.

Women lie, men lie, but the energy never lies. One thing I've noticed when I meet people is that no matter how great the conversation may be, the tell-tell sign to their personality is the vibe I pick up. Human interactions rely on vibes and energy. You can leave a social setting feeling the love, anxiety, or the overall goodness from a room. The reason for this is because energy is more real than words and smiles. No one can fake energy, no matter what words they use to mask it. The problem is most people are unaware, so they rely on what people say versus how those people make them feel. It's like someone loves bomb you, and you hear the word, but you cannot seem to feel the loving energy. In this chapter, I will identify the components that make up your energy field, which can be measured as an arm's length away from a person's body.

Vow to yourself today that you will choose to see past the illusion of 10-year friendships, friendliness, and flowery words. And want to feel more than you see with the naked eye. Feelings are the indicators of what energy is to us. Master your emotions because they attract situations, they create circumstances, and they influence the world around you. Now I'm sure you feel like emotions aren't controllable, I'm only human. I'm not saying suppress feelings I'm saying don't allow them to become dominant in your vibration, allow the feelings to come and go. Do not hold onto it by identifying with it and affirming with words that you are angry, instead say that you feel anger and break it into parts with reasoning to describe why you think that way. From there, the emotion will subside.

Think of the infant that has a temper tantrum, and he is so young he hasn't mastered his energy, and his frustration takes over his entire body, and he falls to the ground screaming, kicking crying and its real chaos. As adults, when we cannot maintain mastery of our human body, we are like a child. An adult emotional tantrum affects their manifestations because the adult has a vast energy-field, so every ripple effect is a wave into the universe. You are powerful.

Energy is what creates the life you desire. It's just as simple as focusing on what you want, and putting action towards it will build up energy in that direction. Then BOOM! You manifest (create) it into reality. Apply this to manifesting a house, dream jobs, love, and being a better you. Everything and anything you want to create or experience in life requires energy. Let us identify what affects your energy field.

Food

The consumption of food is the basis of energy. Diet affects the brain, the immune system, emotions, and overall appearance. People who practice gluttony stuff themselves with so much food they can't think clearly and people who don't eat healthily are incapacitated. Food is energy. We only need energy to survive. Food receives its power from the sun, and we then consume it to receive the energy and distribute it to the organs in our body. The process and the purpose of the food served is to be fuel and give us nutrients to operate our bodies properly. Eat and be well. High vibration foods are foods that come from the ground or the trees or food that sits in the sun, and those are all edible — not rabbits, cows, and animals. Vegetarian and vegan lifestyles are a fantastic route to vibrate high. You will be in better moods, making better decisions, and your meditations will have clarity. This lifestyle requires discipline and control of your taste buds. There are so many options out there now to be a vegetarian or vegan in 2020 is a blessing.

What you put in your body becomes apart of your body, therefore, affecting the energy that you give off. You are what you eat or consume. While this phrase is common, it is also commonly overlooked. It's time we all take responsibility for our health and become consciously aware of the effects the food we eat have on our energy. Not just to be physically healthy but to be mentally fit and energetically healthy. What you put in your body becomes apart of your body, therefore, affecting the energy that you give off. Low vibrations generally include junk food, alcohol, and red meat. This food 15b 1bv ` s` affects your mood and your thoughts. Emotions and thoughts affect your energy. Can you see the domino effect happening here? For example, if your consuming junk food that has artificial flavors and high sugar counts, you might feel down. Sugar is a depressant, and a person who is depressed is giving off low vibes. Alcohol is low vibration and affects your mood and behavior. Want to see for yourself? Take time to notice the reactions of people when they are consuming alcohol and junk food.

Music

Are you surprised? No, don't be music affects your energy field. That's because music has its frequency. That frequency can influence your energy field. Want to feel happy? What song comes to mind? Cold play is one of my favorite groups, but the parachutes album makes me feel sad. The music we allow ourselves to hear affects our hearts and our minds and pushes the energy around in a manipulative way. It can be good or bad, depending on the song. Hertz is the way you measure the energy level a musical sound is affecting you. We should check the hertz in a song the way we check ingredients on the back of a box of snacks. A lot of music artists are aware of how specific beats influence behavior, rappers, rockers, composers of all kinds. Think about how classical music makes you feel, and the production has peaceful tones, and so does jazz. It gives you a feeling of relaxation. Good vibes aren't hard to notice; we are just comfortable in are undisciplined lives. Sound is a wave, and it has length, and it can inspire you to win or fail, love, or hate. Guard your ear gates and pay attention to the sounds you accept into your energy field.

Sexual Intercourse

Sexual intercourse is a vast energy manipulator. Sex is an act that requires you to exert energy, so it very different from being in the receptive mode with food or music. There is a noticeable exchange going on here, and it transfers a person's entire energy field onto their sexual partner. So what happens is you will pick up whatever your sex partner has in there field. It is much different from a handshake or a hug, which is also considered physical contact. The difference is the energy exchanged in a handshake, or a hug can reject it, unlike sex, where it is automatic. The danger here is if a person is dealing with sadness, anger, or any low vibration emotions, you will contract this. Also, if their body is lacking any energy like love or positivity and possess it, they will drain you. That's why with some sexual partners, you feel energized with and light-hearted and happy afterward, and others leave you feeling tired, empty, and drained of your energy. Sex workers often go crazy mentally because they are exchanging energy from strangers everyday. Pimps are aware that a prostitute can only last as a worker for so long before she completely loses her mind, due to frivolous energy exchange. Sex trafficking is a sick business because they force women to exchange their energy as a form of slavery. Protect your sacred sexual energy. It affects your entire system and affects how you operate in the world. You will be different from your usual self. It is wise to review at least the person you choose to exchange life force. On a positive note, sex with the right person who is energetically healthy can increase your life force. It will have positive effects, your skin will glow, and your mood lighter, boost your immune system. Everything is good.

Water

Water is life. It allows life's energy to flow and increase. If you are using lots of energy and you drink water, it will replenish your supply. Water is a magical liquid, and your body is majority water. So if you are energy and majority water, it is safe to say that water is your best friend. It's equivalent to oil on rust. It is needed for us to move and exist. Have you ever experienced a charlie horse on your leg? It comes from not drinking enough water, your muscles tense up and it causes you great pain. Just consider your leg is like a rusted part in need of some oil, the same with dry skin, chapped lips, etc. To vibrate higher, drink lots of water. You are water, and the body (energy) can only exist without water for a week. And more than three weeks without food. Water has more power. It has oxygen, and it is composed of the two major things we need as humans.

SEVEN
Tools: Amplify Your Energy

Visualization is a great tool to channel your energy towards specific goals that you want to accomplish. It's just like daydreaming but more intentional. From vision comes form. Vision is something everyONE uses to build their company; it all starts with a picture in your head. You put the pieces of the picture together bit by piece over time. It is the vision that sets the foundation for all dreams to come to life.

The human brain doesn't know the difference between what's real or something you visualize. The eyes are a window to your soul, so be mindful of the things you watch and the visions you allow your mind to see.

Visualizing is a great way to align with your future, and it will always be a way to find out what is next for your life. It is you dreaming of your future and realize what can be true to you focus on, you find that this is not about making things up, but when you align your thoughts with your deepest desires. You will get a glimpse into the future, and that is the picture of what your life can and will be like if you follow your intuition and continues to guide yourself down the path of least resistance.

Visions are from the creator, and people visualize their lovers, their new ideas, and even things that don't exist in the present. From vision comes form if you choose to work at it — all of the visions that you wish to have you can practice. With high intention, there will be more than enough room for perfection. You will begin to see what has always been there. So this is how it works, you close your eyes and try to envision the very best version of yourself. The subconscious mind knows exactly how this version of you looks like you just have to call it up and there will be a picture of you that will pop up in your head. Then envision yourself. Doing things and living the life that your future self will do. Then you must accept in your heart that this vision can happen, and it will be so.

Some visions you can share with others, and some visions are private. You will know which is which. Visualization can be a daily or weekly habit, and it allows you to connect with your future self. You are the most beautiful reflection, and when you accept that, you can then quickly take the beauty of what tomorrow brings you.

Crystals

Crystals are another great tool to amplify your energy. Crystals possess their energy field, and when a person has mastered that, they can then work with the gems to increase it. Crystals are precious stones that some people consider to be a rock. People sometimes associate crystals with black magic and witchcraft and all sorts of things. Crystals are neutral; they do not belong to any specific group, but they can be used by all who choose to tap into their healing energy. The purpose of the crystal stones is to heal your emotions, protect your energy, and attract specific energies to you. What else on this earth is as phenomenal as colored stones found on the planet. When using crystals, be sure to manage how your body reacts to specific stones. There is one called the tiger's eye, which has the healing properties for mental health, which is excellent for all humans and helps us to think better. An infamous one is an amethyst, which is remarkable for clarity. There are many others that aid in communication, prosperity, love, and happiness. Notice I said support not create, this is not magic. You must be energetically ready for what you wish to amplify in your life.

Taking care of your stones is similar to how you take care of babies, wash them in water give them sun and hold them in your hand to keep them in tune with your vibe.

You will be amazed at what the stones will add to your life and take away. If you have tourmaline, these repel negative energies. Watch the people that will disappear out of your life. You can make plans to hang, but something will always come up and interfere with your meetups. It will prevent you from being around people that secretly might not be best for you. Hold on to the rose quartz and notice all of the love that enters your life through strangers, old friends, animals, and your enjoyment of self. Your life will improve following the effort you make to exert the energy you wish to receive.

If your personality is mean and nasty and your choice is to be that way daily, expect your crystal to mysteriously disappear, fall out of your pocket, or be misplaced. It cannot amplify what never existed in your vibration.

You can gift crystals to others when you are led to do so. Only give it away when you have received all of what it offers you. If your crystal ever breaks in half because you dropped it, that means giving the other half to the first person that comes to mind.

Teas

Tea lovers this for you! Teas are herbs. They come from the earth. Tea herbs since ancient times in history have been a standard beverage. You are always best when healed, and in a relaxed state, this makes you more of a pleasure to be around. There are teas related to each energy center in your body, and this is a form of self-care.

Root Chakra- Ginger tea, dandelion root
Sacral Chakra- calendula tea, hibiscus
Solar Plexus- Rosemary tea, cinnamon
Heart Chakra- Jasmine tea, hawthorn berry
Throat Chakra- Red clover tea, lemon
3rd eye Chakra- Mint tea, lemon
Crown Chakra- Lavender tea, lotus root

Chakras

These are energy centers in the body, and we give them the name chakras to identify them. They each work on the part of our limbic system. Which focuses on instincts and moods, meaning our basic emotions. When you heal every part of this system, you become whole. Chakras are the energy centers that allow us to be more compassionate, understanding, courageous, and loving. There are personal truths you will find in each one of these gateways. Please don't force yourself to unlock these parts of you allow it to happen naturally. Take it one day at a time; healing is a process. Some chakras rely on others to heal first before you can work on what's next. For example, the heart chakra is the key to unlocking all of the other chakras because it purifies your intentions and allows you to love yourself and others unconditionally.

Heart Chakra Affirmations

I choose joy, compassion, and love
I love myself unconditionally and offer the same to others
My heart is free from all the wounds of the past
I know my own emotions, and I accept whatever form they take
I forgive others, and I forgive myself

When you meditate on this, you will feel so much release, crying tears of joy and truly feel like your true self. There are parts of you that you never knew needed healing that will. We all repress parts of ourselves due to trauma. This repressed pain triggers us, and we don't even know why. When we are still dealing with pain in our limbic system, this is a blocked chakra. The heart chakra is the only chakra I will explain in this book. It is the most important and will activate all other chakras to begin their healing process. Love is the key.

The heart is the most potent source of electromagnetic energy. Your heart's energy field is 100 times greater than your brain. That's why it's important to do what you love and love what you do. In your work, that love you give comes back to you. It is karmic law. Love karma returns to us in all types of beautiful ways. Give with a loving heart, speak with a warm tone, and love thy neighbor as you love yourself. The energy you possess will be contagious, and your life will be sweet.

EIGHT
Praise & Worship

Praise and worship are done all over the world across nations. We all call it different things, but ultimately we are honoring God, the creator, and the God of the universe, who is the higher power of life here on earth. It is a sign of respect and gratitude, and it shows appreciation, and those who participate often receive blessings, not because they expect it in exchange but because they're pure in heart. God can tell when we are praising from the right place. The quickest way to receive in this world is through praise. Praise is almost a lost art amongst Millenials who have decided that it was something for the elderly and older adults. We fail to realize that it is the ultimate gift to be alive, and praise is the ultimate way to say " thank you." The vibration of a grateful heart draws to you more things to be thankful in life. With the combination of these key components, you will increase your energy field to higher levels. All over the world, people lift their hands to acknowledge the higher power and show themselves as servants to the world. We are all here to appreciate and love. No one should see themselves as excluded or too important to engage in praise. It is the law of the land that has been forgotten and overlooked in the past years. Praise his holy name and watch the wondrous miracles that happen for you.

Move forward fearlessly and let go of what others will think of you. In your life, you are accountable for your energy field. Don't be ashamed of what others might think and how this might look to your peers. None of them matter, because half of those people will not be around to witness your first million-dollar check. Your life will continue to elevate, bringing you in contact with new people and new energy, and people will come and go. The only thing that will be a constant is your spirit and the God you serve. He is always present even when no one else is around.

Now, if you are new to worship, it might seem weird in the beginning. Over time it will create a personal relationship between you and the creator. The more you praise, it will become natural to you, and you'll develop our style. He is the only one watching you, so recognize this as an intimate moment. When you adopt this practice in your spiritual life, this becomes apart of who you are. The goal transforms your life into one that is not religious but spiritual, meaning as you feel lead to praise naturally.

Dancing is included in praise, as dancing raises your vibration. Move your body! Clap your hands! Energy is an act of motion, so body movement is an important step. I often praise with worship music by lifting my hands in up and down movements. I worship with my body by jumping up and down and twirling in circles, moving with grace and excitement. Utilize this to be grateful for all that he has done for you. Fills up your heart with appreciation, focusing on all of the good in life. It is good to do this multiple times during the week. Think of praise as a party, a praise party with you, and the divine. There are only songs of holiness and dance moves that aren't provocative. Have fun; this is about being happy! You can praise with a group of people, your pet, or by yourself. Praise is not always about seriousness. No alcohol is involved or smoking; it is not a worldly party; it is about a moment to dance with God. You can two-step your way around the house.

Anything giving appreciation or glory and joy is praise. It is his due right to receive our worship we pray to ask, we pray to talk, we meditate to listen, but those are all not in honor of his presence in our life; those are just mechanisms for living a holy life. Praise is precisely what we should give on a daily. God is pleased when we offer up our energy to God in the form of dance, which is movement (kinetic energy) with a song which is vibration praise and gratitude, which is positive thoughts and emotions towards his grace. It should be the first thing we dedicate ourselves to in the morning because we acknowledge that he woke us up and gave us another day to live and seek our purpose here on earth. God has amazing energy, and we have to be in alignment with his path for us to truly receive the good we deserve to be good faithful servants. God is the creator of the heavens and the earth, the galaxy, and the universe. He is mighty. It is the very least we can do in our little world that exists. Do not let the time spent on this earth be in vain, meaning-focused on us and our goals, our lifestyle, and material possessions that up space leave room for his presence.

The return you receive from praise is healing, and praise will heal depression, sorrow, and a negative mindset. It is because to praise God is to bring his energy into your surroundings. And the spirit of God is holy and clean and therefore purifies all those who are in the midst. He will clean you and wipe your slate clean. This is the power of what honoring God does to our bodies and minds. Do not undermine this practice. It will bring you to tears of joy, and the tears will feel so peaceful because we hold so much in to hide from friends, family, and the world. When we step into the presence of God as our heavenly spiritual father, we began to feel vulnerable and open. We can be real in front of him, so often you experience emotions that have denied. It is safe to be yourself in his glory. It is in those moments you will know that he is the way the truth and the light.

Praise will move you up into a new place. Praise God before you receive what it is you want in life. If you wish to heal, praise him while you are sick, and you will experience immunity. If you are poor, praise him when you are without and you will soon have. If you are lonely, praise him in solitude and you will soon enjoy the company of others. Praise to change the circumstances you currently experience. It is a conduit of change and improvement. Praise before and after and always watch the miracles flow to you in divine timing, so have faith and patience.

Another practice that you should do sparingly is fasting. Fasting is another way to honor God. Fasting is a sacrifice that requires focus and intention. People can learn new things and experience breakthroughs within their life due to fasting and resisting the urge to feed ourselves. We enjoy food, but we only need it for energy to survive. So when we sacrifice our urge for food enjoyment, we show God how serious we are about our request. It is our way of showing discipline and our way of offering something to him, "desire." Fasting is excellent for many reasons, for health and digestive purposes, and for the opportunity to be a clear channel to God and his voice. A day spent fasting should be consumed with prayer and meditation, to talk and listen and ponder on the thoughts we receive in those moments. God is pleased with fasting and it is through fasting; he sees our true nature and heart. It is good and it will connect you with divine energy.

Fasting requires mental discipline, and if you are following the chapters guide, you should have developed more control of your thoughts and body urges. You can prepare to engage in fasting as a holy practice when you are in control of your energy. It is all about your capacity to be strong for yourself, and it is only in strength that you can resist food, drink, and desire. How long can you fast? Some can last for weeks with the assistance of lemon water, and there are fasting techniques that require you to prepare weeks in advance slowly decreasing your food intake and eating healthier and cleaning up your diet with more vegetables and fruits you will prepare each organ to regenerate and all of the cells in our body will renew — overall creating anew version of your body makeup. God will recreate you. We don't come into his grace to be the same person we come to be revived. At the end of our fasting period, we should slowly get back to eating and don't eat the same unhealthy foods as before because then your just going back to the old you. Develop a new diet to sustain the new body you have created and this will allow you to walk in the world as a better version of you! Be made whole.

Lastly, this is the part where you ask Christ to come into your life, and you do this not because you want to be a Christian but because you want his loving energy to be in your world. You want him there with you, walking down the street, making things happen, covering you in your new body with a new mindset. You want him present to orchestrate miracles and to shield you from harm. Christ's energy is divine God sent him for that purpose don't allow religion and Christianity to stand between you and Jesus Christ. Only ask him to come into your life when you are ready to be different and love different and walk in your spiritual path. He will be more than happy to walk with you because he loves us and that is the energy that allowed him to die on the cross.

He conquered death and fear and all of the feelings that humans experience for the children of humanity. He is always ready to be in your life, so whenever it is clever, invite him in. This book isn't about converting you to any type of religion; it is allowing you to become aware of your spirit. Your spirit is existing in an energy-based grid. It doesn't matter how people view this concept. The experience is the only teacher; it is the only thing that will show you what's real and what's not. I started my spiritual journey as an atheist, and I found myself, my spirit, and God in the process. Unlearning was an essential step to learning. Jesus saves, and this is his mantra. He wants to be known as the savor. Sink or swim in life but remember that your spirit lives on into eternity. If this is understood, then you won't have to die to come to this realization you can realize it now, and that will create your heaven here on earth. Live consciously now. Find who you are now. Be aware of energy today. It is only now that exist tomorrow is just a fantasy who knows if it will come. The now is where it all happens for you.

NINE
Mastery

The importance of mastering who you are is so that you can be added to the list of conscious people. Conscious life is a life that is truly lived. It is all about creating more for yourself. Could you imagine a future that is filled with a God-conscious world? It would be a dream to walk outside and see common sense being common. In the creation of life that you mold for yourself, you are indirectly creating a world for others too. It would be selfish to only see this as a journey affected by no one else, but it is affecting everyone you are in contact with. Your energy is a reflection of your friends, family, and associates. If you can make it beautiful, you will be sharing it with everyone that you come in contact with. You will no longer say you didn't know. You can't unlearn what you have read in this book. It will stick with you for as long as you choose to apply it to your everyday life.

Change, grow, evolve, resist, exchange be whole. These are the six commandments that I decided to commit myself to. The lord is my witness that it was not easy, but it was so much fun trusting God and trusting myself and trusting life. It was fun learning to manage my emotions and cultivate more joy and happiness in my life with intent. Choosing to love yourself every day is not a task; it is a birthright. It is on this day that you will receive all of the things that make you whole. It is in this story that you can find your story.